# THE WORLD AT WAR
# WORLD WAR II

# The Blitz on Britain

Heinemann
LIBRARY

. . . . . . . . . Brian Williams

**www.heinemann.co.uk/library**
Visit our website to find out more information about **Heinemann Library** books.

To order:
☎ Phone 44 (0) 1865 888066
▤ Send a fax to 44 (0) 1865 314091
▯ Visit the Heinemann Bookshop at www.heinemann.co.uk/library to browse our catalogue and order online.

First published in Great Britain by Heinemann Library, Halley Court, Jordan Hill, Oxford OX2 8EJ, part of Harcourt Education.
Heinemann is a registered trademark of Harcourt Education Ltd.

Editorial: Andrew Farrow and Dan Nunn
Design: Lucy Owen and Tokay Interactive Ltd (www.tokay.co.uk)
Picture Research: Hannah Taylor and Sally Claxton
Production: Duncan Gilbert

Originated by Repro Multi Warna
Printed and bound in China by WKT Company Limited

The paper used to print this book comes from sustainable resources.

ISBN 0 431 10376 3
10 09 08 07 06
10 9 8 7 6 5 4 3 2 1

**British Library Cataloguing in Publication Data**
Williams, Brian, 1943–
  The Blitz on Britain. – (World at war. World War II)
  1. World War, 1939–1945 – Aerial operations, German – Juvenile literature 2. World War, 1939–1945 – Campaigns – Great Britain – Juvenile literature 3. Great Britain – History – Bombardment, 1944–1945 – Juvenile literature
  I. Title
  940.5'4211
A full catalogue record for this book is available from the British Library.

**Acknowledgements**
The publishers would like to thank the following for permission to reproduce photographs:

Art Archive p. **19 top** (Imperial War Museum/ Eileen Tweedy); Corbis pp. **4** (Bettmann), **6**, **7 bottom** (Bettmann), **7 top** (Hulton Deutsch Collection), **8** (Hulton Deutsch Collection), **9** (Hulton Deutsch Collection), **13** (Hulton Deutsch Collection), **14 bottom**, **15 top** (Hulton Deutsch Collection), **17** (Hulton Deutsch Collection), **18 top** (Hulton Deutsch Collection), **23 bottom** (Hulton Deutsch Collection), **25**, **28** (Hulton Deutsch Collection); Getty Images pp. **10** (Hulton Archive), **16** (Hulton Archive), **24** (Hulton Archive), **27 top** (Hulton Archive); Imperial War Museum pp. **14 top**, **20**, **22**, **23 top**; National Archives pp. **11**, **15 bottom**; Topfoto.co.uk pp. **5**, **11 bottom**, **12**, **19 bottom**, **21**, **26** (HIP/The Lord Price Collection), **27 bottom**, **27 middle**; TRH Pictures p. **18 bottom**.

Cover photograph of people being rescued after a Luftwaffe bombing raid on London in 1940 reproduced with permission of AKG Images.

# CONTENTS

Some words are shown in bold, **like this**. You can find out what they mean by looking in the glossary.

# THE BLITZ ON BRITAIN

World War II (1939–1945) was the first war in which mass air attacks were made on towns and cities. Experts in the 1930s believed that bombing could destroy cities, and would cause people to panic. In 1940, German planes began raids on British cities to force Britain to surrender. These attacks from the air became known as the Blitz.

## The war begins

On 1 September 1939, the **Nazi** leader, Adolf Hitler, sent German armies to invade Poland. Britain and France then went to war to help Poland. Other countries, such as Australia and Canada, joined in too. In Poland, German tanks and soldiers were backed up by the German air force, the Luftwaffe. Poland was quickly overrun. By June 1940, the German *Blitzkrieg* (see panel) had swept through Denmark, Norway, Belgium, Holland, and France. Britain found itself alone in Europe.

▲ German bombers such as this Ju-87 Stuka attacked towns and troops as German armies overran Poland and France.

## What does Blitz mean?

**Blitz** is short for *Blitzkrieg*, a German word meaning "lightning war". It was used in Britain to describe the bombing of towns and cities.

| September 1939 | April 1940 | May 1940 |
| --- | --- | --- |
| The German Luftwaffe destroys the Polish air force. | Germany invades Denmark and Norway. | Germany invades Belgium, Holland, and France. In France, the Luftwaffe destroys many British as well as French planes. |

## The German plan

Adolf Hitler hoped Britain would agree to a peace deal. But Britain's prime minister, Winston Churchill, retorted that the country would never surrender. While German armies waited in France, Luftwaffe planes flew to attack Britain.

The plan was to bomb British ports and ships and to destroy Britain's war industry and air force. The German navy could not defeat the bigger British navy unless the Luftwaffe could control the skies. After they had destroyed the British Royal Air Force (RAF), German **bombers** would be able to drive British warships from the English Channel. Then the British would have to surrender or be invaded.

The Germans did not set out to bomb Britain's cities – the RAF was their first target. However, Hitler's plan was foiled by the RAF's gallant fighter pilots. In the summer of 1940, they fought off the German bombers and won the Battle of Britain. The Luftwaffe began to attack British cities instead. The Blitz began.

▲ German planes attacked shipping in the English Channel, to cripple Britain by cutting off its supplies of food and war materials.

5

**July–September 1940**
The Battle of Britain: RAF fighters defend airfields and **radar** stations in southern Britain against the Luftwaffe.

**September 1940**
The Luftwaffe starts bombing London. The plan is to spread terror and force Britain to surrender.

**October 1940**
By October 1940, around 1,300 German planes have been shot down in the Battle of Britain. Hitler abandons his plan to invade, but the Blitz continues.

# The Battle of Britain

During the Battle of Britain in the summer of 1940, German bombers, escorted by fighters, attacked RAF fighter bases. RAF fighter pilots took off to fight the enemy in air battles called **dogfights**.

## A day that changed things

On 15 September 1940, German pilots launched their biggest attack so far. Alerted by radar, the RAF sent over 20 **squadrons** of fighters into action – more than ever before. In the afternoon, even more German planes appeared. British Prime Minister Winston Churchill asked an RAF commander how many fighters were in reserve. "None", came the reply. Yet, by evening, the Luftwaffe had lost more than 50 planes. Two days later, Hitler gave up any hopes of invading Britain. The first part of the air battle over Britain had been won.

## In the News

On 21 September 1940, the Lord Mayor of London made a radio broadcast to New York. He said, "Today London stands as the very bulwark [protection] of civilization and freedom. These streets of my city will be defended to the last." Mayor La Guardia of New York City replied, "Bravo, London ...We are praying for you. Thumbs up, London."

## Eyewitness

"... at 15,000 feet we saw thirty Heinkels [bombers] supported by fifty Me109s [fighters] 4,000 feet above them and twenty Me110s to a flank, approaching us from above. We turned and climbed, flying in the same direction as the bombers ... so each man had a view of the enemy."

*An RAF fighter pilot, 15 September 1940*

▶ Britain had one special advantage in the Battle of Britain. It had more than 20 top-secret radar stations. Radar gave the RAF around 20 minutes' warning of German aircraft crossing the coast to bomb airfields.

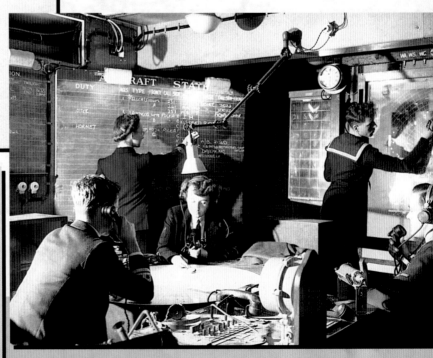

"Never in the field of human conflict was so much owed by so many to so few."

*Winston Churchill, Britain's prime minister, praised the bravery of the pilots who fought in the Battle of Britain.*

▲ RAF Hurricane pilots "scramble" to attack German bombers. The RAF had captured a German Bf-109 fighter, and thought RAF planes were better. The Spitfire flew at over 350 mph (563 kph), and fired eight machine guns. The sturdy Hurricane was slower, but also had eight guns.

▲ The wreck of a German Messerschmitt Bf-109. Most Luftwaffe planes were shot down by RAF fighters, but some were hit by ground fire from guns.

▼ The table below compares the approximate number of planes each side had available in May 1940. British bombers were not directly involved in the Battle of Britain and so are not included here.

## Air power in May 1940

| Luftwaffe facing Britain | RAF in Britain |
| --- | --- |
| 1,200 medium bombers – mostly Do-17s, He-111s, and Ju-88s | 300 Hurricane fighters |
| 280 Ju-87 dive bombers | 228 Spitfire fighters |
| 760 single-engined Bf-109 fighters | 30 two-seat Defiant fighters |
| 220 twin-engined Bf-110 fighters | 72 twin-engined Blenheim fighters |
| **Total:** 2460 bombers and fighters | **Total:** 630 fighters |

# CITIES UNDER FIRE

**In September 1940, the Luftwaffe stopped attacking airfields and started dropping bombs on Britain's biggest city, London.**

Looking up on 7 September, Londoners in streets and gardens saw black dots in the sky – around 300 German bombers following the snaking course of the River Thames. Then they heard the sound of explosions, and saw black smoke rising. In this one raid, in daylight, over 300 people were killed and 1,300 seriously injured.

## London's Blitz

To avoid RAF fighters, German bombers soon turned to night raids. The bombing of London continued almost nightly into 1941. Huge fires raged as warehouses packed with sugar, timber, paint, and other inflammable materials burned fiercely. The poorer districts close to the docks of the River Thames were hardest hit. Whole streets of houses were flattened. Across the city, historic buildings were reduced to rubble, but St Paul's Cathedral survived among the smoke and flames. German radio reported that crowds terrified by the bombs had rioted, but this **propaganda** was not true.

▲ Coventry had little defence as over 400 German bombers flew over the city. The Blitz reduced most of the medieval cathedral to a pile of rubble.

## Cities under attack

On 14 November 1940, the Luftwaffe bombed the Midlands city of Coventry. This attack shocked many people. Coventry had factories, but it was not thought to be a major target. That winter, other cities were bombed, including Birmingham, Manchester, Glasgow, and Belfast. So too were ports such as Bristol, Swansea, and Liverpool.

| **24–25 August 1940** | **7 September 1940** | **14 November 1940** |
| --- | --- | --- |
| RAF planes bomb the German capital city, Berlin. Hitler is furious and threatens revenge. | German planes raid London. On a fine Saturday afternoon, Londoners are surprised to see swarms of bombers overhead. | Coventry is raided by over 400 German bombers. More than 500 people are killed. |

> ▶ Many bombing raids were against military targets like this aircraft factory.

> ▼ This map shows how the German Luftwaffe used bases in occupied Europe to launch raids across Britain.

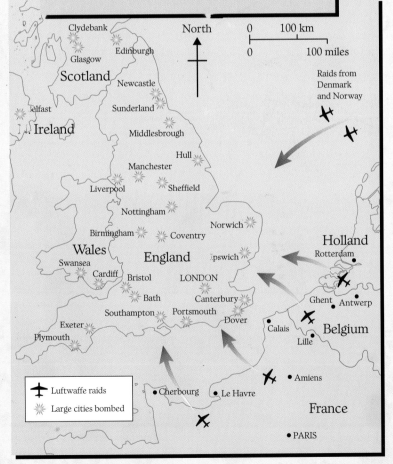

## Eyewitness

*This is how a London firefighter saw the scene in London's East India Dock on 7 September 1940.*

"Wherever the eye could see, vast sheets of flame and a terrific roar ... The fire [at a warehouse] was so huge that we could do little more than make a feeble attempt to put it out ... a crowd of women and children were streaming away from the danger area, carrying bundles over their shoulders ... a flock of pigeons kept circling overhead almost all night. They seemed lost ..."

**12 December 1940**

The industrial city of Sheffield is bombed for nine hours.

**1–7 May 1941**

German planes bomb Merseyside, leaving more than 50,000 people homeless in and around Liverpool.

**10–11 May 1941**

More than 1,400 people are killed in London. The House of Commons, Westminster Abbey, and the British Museum are all hit.

# Blackouts and balloons

Even before the war, Britain had made plans for **civil defence** against **air raids**. Bomb-proof **air raid shelters** were built. To cope with the Blitz, extra firefighters and ambulance crews were needed. Air Raid Precautions (ARP) wardens, men and women, patrolled the streets. Rescue and repair teams worked tirelessly to save lives and clear away rubble as more bombs fell.

The blackout made it harder for enemy planes to find targets. Streetlights were switched off and people drew dark curtains across windows, so that no light showed. Everywhere was very dark.

▼ Thousands of barrage balloons floated above towns and key targets, such as factories. The gas balloons were flown from long wire cables. They stopped German planes flying low over a target. Some bombers crashed into the balloon cables.

## Defence tactics

- Big guns were used to shoot down enemy bombers.

- Anti-aircraft (AA or "ack-ack") guns were used to force bombers to fly too high for accurate bombing.

- Fighter planes chased and shot down some bombers.

- By 1941, RAF night fighter pilots had radar to guide them in the darkness.

▲ A decoy (fake) plane sits in a field, awaiting enemy attack. Fake targets like this were set up to trick Luftwaffe bomber crews into bombing the wrong places. Fake lights looked like roads or airfield runways. There were decoy towns and ports, too.

## Eyewitness

"You have no idea how dark is dark, unless you have experienced a night with no moon, fog, and the blackout."

*Doreen May, remembering the blackout in Britain. There were many accidents on dark nights, with no streetlights. Cars had special dimmed headlamps.*

◀ Searchlights, often operated by women of the Auxiliary Territorial Service (ATS), shone into the night sky. The searchlight beams were aimed at enemy planes, to help anti-aircraft gunners shoot them down.

# DEATH AND DESTRUCTION

**The Nazis hoped the Blitz would destroy Britain's ability to fight. They hoped that killing people and wrecking homes would weaken morale.**

Luftwaffe boss Hermann Goering assured Hitler that "terror bombing", night after night, would cause panic across Britain. The Luftwaffe would destroy homes, hospitals, shops, factories, and railways. Normal life would collapse and the British would be forced to make peace. But the British were much tougher than Goering thought.

▲ A bomb fell roughly 20 metres (65 feet) in front of this London bus as it travelled through the Blitz. Luckily, the driver escaped to tell his story.

## Find the target

It was also very difficult for the Luftwaffe to bomb accurately. As well as maps, German bomber crews followed special radio beams to find their targets. However, bomb-aiming was not easy from 5,000 metres (16,404 feet) above the ground. Bombs in the 1940s were not guided, like missiles today, but often fell haphazardly. They were dropped in groups, known as **sticks**, landing one after the other. People could sometimes hear bombs coming. They joked grimly that you didn't hear the bomb that would hit you.

## High explosive

Most bombs were packed with high explosives, and exploded on impact. A direct hit from a bomb would demolish a house and kill everyone in it. The blast would also wreck houses on either side. Bomb blasts could kill people with no trace of an injury. However, many people were injured by flying shrapnel (fragments of metal) or splinters of wood and glass. Others were buried beneath bricks, girders, and roof timbers.

**12**

| September 1940 | September 1940 | 2 January 1941 |
| --- | --- | --- |
| Southampton is hit by 2,000 bombs. Over half the houses in the city are damaged. | The British government orders men to "fire watch" for up to 48 hours every month. Women too become fire-watchers. | Cardiff's worst raid. Rescuers dig out a six-year-old boy buried under the stairs of his wrecked home. He guides them by singing "God Save the King". |

## Fire bombs

**Incendiary** (fire) bombs were small, but packed with chemicals such as phosphorus that burst into flame. Incendiary bombs started small fires that quickly spread to fuel tanks, factories, and warehouses.

## Bombs that did not go off

A delayed-action bomb did not go off at once. It had a timer inside, set to explode hours after it landed. It was a booby trap. But many ordinary bombs failed to explode simply because they did not work properly. Unexploded bombs (UXBs) were very dangerous.

## The Baedeker raids

Attacks on historic towns such as Canterbury and Bath were known as "Baedeker" raids, after a series of tourist guide books called the *Baedeker Guides*. People said German pilots used the books to find their targets.

◄ Each unexploded bomb (UXB) had to be uncovered, its casing opened, and its explosive made harmless. Army bomb disposal experts were very brave, risking their lives daily. Many were killed.

| 3 January 1941 | 21–29 April 1941 | May 1941 |
|---|---|---|
| Bristol firefighters face an extra problem: freezing weather turns water from fire hoses to ice. | In five raids over nine nights, 750 bombers pound the naval base and city of Plymouth. | The east coast port of Hull suffers its 49th raid since 1940. Over two nights, 46 rest centres care for 16,000 homeless people. |

# Fighting the fires

Air raids started countless numbers of fires. Hundreds of men and women "fire-watchers" kept watch from the tops of buildings, to spot the incendiary bombs responsible.

Firefighters often battled so close to blazing buildings that the fierce heat turned the water gushing from their hoses to steam. When water pipes were smashed, not even a river could supply enough water to quench the flames. Then exhausted firefighters had to watch buildings burn to the ground.

During the Blitz, more than 800 firefighters were killed and 7,000 seriously injured. Among them were "auxiliary" firefighters, who had left their jobs to become wartime firefighters.

▼ Firefighters fought the flames with water hoses, from the ground and from ladders high above the street. "On big Blitz nights, when there are any number of fires …, you wonder how they'll get them all out … From time to time the smoke billows up and you can see nothing below you. Then you feel horribly alone …" remembered one London firefighter.

▲ A fire bomb could be put out with a shovel of sand, or by squirting it with water from a small stirrup pump. Quick action could prevent a big fire taking hold.

> ▶ This is a German pilot's view of London during the Blitz.

## In the News

"In normal times, a fire requiring 30 pumps is a very big fire. On 7 September, there were nine fires in London rating over 100 pumps. The biggest, at Woolwich Arsenal [a key centre for making guns and explosives] was rated at 200 pumps. Many firemen were at work for 40 hours ..."

*From a British government report on the London Blitz, 1940*

> ▼ The British government issued posters to alert people to the dangers from fires.

**HOW TO FIGHT THE FIRE-BOMB**

A MINISTRY OF INFORMATION
EXHIBITION

FREE

## Eyewitness

Firefighters were often the first to find the bodies of people killed by the bombs. Les Bennett, a Middlesbrough firefighter in 1942, remembered finding "three lads wrapped round a lamp post; they'd been out watching the bombing and been caught by the blast. They were all dead."

15

# TAKING SHELTER

Civil defence meant providing air raid shelters for people. The government also encouraged people to evacuate (leave) the towns and cities that were in most danger of being bombed.

▶ Two evacuee children meet their new "parent". The country was a shock to some town children. One child was surprised to see carrots fresh from the soil, and said, "ours grow in tins, they aren't dirty like that".

By October 1939, over a million people, mostly mothers and children, had been **evacuated** in trains and buses from the cities to the countryside. Children sent to live with host families in the country were known as "evacuees". A small number of children went overseas, to America or Canada. To protect against poison-gas attacks, 38 million **gas masks** were given out, including special masks for babies.

## Air raid shelters

Most people did not want to move from their homes – many evacuees came back to the cities after a few weeks. Those who stayed needed air raid shelters, and advice about what to do when **sirens** sounded an air raid warning. The government built public air raid shelters – the biggest, at Tilbury east of London, could hold over 15,000 people. But mass shelters became dirty and smelly. Many people preferred to stay at home.

## Advice for evacuees

In 1938, the parents of London schoolchildren were sent letters telling them what children should take when evacuated. The list included:

- washing things
- clothes, including socks, outdoor shoes, and a raincoat
- a games kit
- a brush and comb
- six stamped postcards for writing home
- card games and a book
- their gas mask.

**1939**

The British government starts issuing Anderson shelters, before war begins. A shelter costs £7 but is free to low-income families (earning less than £5 a week).

**September 1940**

London Underground stations are taken over at night by shelterers. Before long, around 150,000 people are sleeping on the platforms.

**October 1940**

Thousands of people shelter each night inside Chislehurst Caves in Kent.

▶ The Anderson shelter was put together inside a pit, dug in the garden. It was cramped inside, but people made their shelters as comfortable as possible.

## Tube and home shelters

Thousands of Londoners sought shelter in the Underground (Tube) railway, sleeping on station platforms. Each regular shelterer had a free ticket, with a number showing a bunk or floor space. Extra spaces were left for "casual" shelterers.

Many families set up a home shelter. This was either an Anderson shelter made of **corrugated steel** in the garden, or a Morrison shelter inside a room.

## Eyewitness

*A London bus conductor was in a shelter, hearing the bombs fall.*

"We counted them [the explosions] ... one, two, three ... seven, eight, nine; they were getting closer ... I could feel my hair going up and up, my hair was standing on end!"

*Luckily for him, the bombs stopped just short of the shelter.*

## Sleepless nights

Air raids meant sleepless nights. Children were roused from their beds and hustled down into the shelter. When the "All-Clear" siren sounded (meaning the bombers had gone), people came out to inspect the damage. They hoped the water, gas, and electricity supplies were still working.

17

**January 1941**

Many people are killed when a bomb falls into the Bank Underground railway station in London.

**March 1941**

The government begins to give the Morrison indoor shelter to families. Over 500,000 are made.

**December 1941**

By the end of the year, 22,000 bunk beds and extra toilets have been provided on Underground stations in London.

# Living in the shelters

For many families, shelter life became routine. There was often a siren alert about 7 p.m., when enemy bombers were sighted. People fixed wooden benches down each side of their Anderson shelter, and put planks across to make beds for their children. Bedclothes were taken into the shelter for the night. Next morning, the blankets were aired around the coal fire in the kitchen.

Air raids were terrifying. There was the noise – air raid sirens wailing, then droning aircraft engines, the thump of exploding bombs, crashes as buildings collapsed, and the "boom-boom" of anti-aircraft guns. Afterwards, there was dust and dirt everywhere, rubble in the street, the smells of burning wood and chemical explosive, and puddles of water from firefighters' hoses.

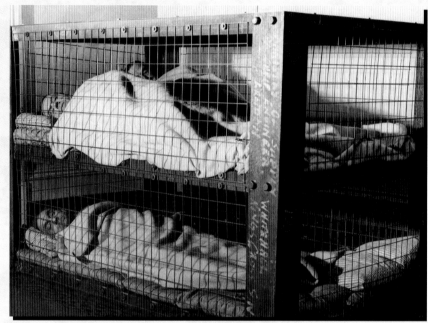

▲ A Morrison shelter. This is how Renée Smith of Wolverhampton described her shelter: "You could either have them in your dining room and use them as a table, or in a bedroom … It was a huge flat piece of steel on four posts. The sides were of steel mesh. … When the alert sounded, we lifted the baby in the carrycot inside and we would get into it … and (hopefully) carry on with our sleep."

## Shelter essentials

Essential shelter items included:

- blankets and pillows

- books and magazines

- games and toys for children

- a handbag containing important documents such as birth certificates and insurance policies

- a torch and candles – some people even had electric fires, toasters, and kettles

- a **wireless** or a wind-up **gramophone.**

◄ Children kept themselves amused with card games and picture books.

▲ Artist Henry Moore drew these pictures of people sheltering in the London Underground during the Blitz. Not everyone went to a shelter. More than half of Londoners said they stayed in bed when they heard the air raid siren!

**AIR RAID PRECAUTIONS**
WHAT TO DO IN
EMERGENCY
6ᴰ

A
COMPREHENSIVE
GUIDE
IN
GRAPHIC NARRATIVE
The Jones Family Sees it Through
by JOHN LANGDON-DAVIES

The Refuge Room
How to Make Garden Trenches
The Construction of Surface Shelters
The Warden Service
Rescue Parties and the Clearance of Debris
The Auxiliary Fire Service
First Aid Posts and Ambulance Services
The Decontamination Squad

# In the News

This typical ARP warden's report was written after an air raid on northern England in April 1942:

"Aircraft attacked at 23.46 hours when four HE [high explosive bombs] fell in a line ... four HE also fell in the river. The first stick of bombs produced 28 killed and 39 injured. Thirty-nine houses were rendered uninhabitable ... 1,156 people were homeless. Seven HE and two UXB [unexploded bombs] fell in the Saltburn area ..."

◄ The British government kept up a flow of advice during the Blitz, urging people to "carry on as normal". Despite fears of mass panic, **morale** was not shattered by night after night of bombing.

# BOMBED OUT

**BOMBED OUT**

**The Blitz destroyed many homes, leaving thousands of people "bombed out" (homeless). Nowhere in Britain was safe.**

One night of bombing could do terrible damage. In 1940 Coventry was hit by 1,400 high-explosive bombs, fifty 900-kilogram (1,984-pound) parachute-bombs or land-mines, and 30,000 fire-bombs. Just one high-explosive bomb could destroy a house and damage others nearby.

The Luftwaffe did not only attack cities and ports. Many small towns were hit by solitary "tip and run" raiders. Stray bombs fell on farms and villages too. Often German planes got rid of bombs while fleeing from pursuing fighters, or released bombs anywhere before flying back to their bases.

## Caring for the homeless

Ambulances took injured victims to hospitals, while rescue teams brought out dead bodies and sifted through the debris to find anyone still alive. Many homeless people were given shelter in church halls and schools, where volunteers served tea, soup, and sandwiches and tried to comfort them.

Homeless families had to be found new homes, often with relatives or friends. Some homes could be patched up. In 1944, the first "prefab" (a prefabricated or factory-built home) went on show. 500,000 new prefabs were needed to rehouse bombed-out families.

▶ The morning after a heavy raid. People cleared up, did what they could to help neighbours, then went to work. Badly damaged buildings were sometimes unsafe and had to be pulled down.

---

**1940**

By winter, rest centres set up to hand out food to Blitz victims have become overcrowded with 25,000 homeless "squatters".

**December 1940**

Volunteer mobile canteens provide for people who have lost their homes, or have no electricity or gas for cooking.

**May 1941**

In Liverpool, 40,000 bombed-out people are found new homes in a week. Some move into "billets" (spare rooms in homes or lodging houses).

◄ Stray bombs landed on villages and farms. Some local people talked about such incidents for years afterwards, remembering "the day the bomb fell ..."

## Picking up the pieces

The day after a raid, survivors picked through the ruins of their homes to rescue toys, photographs, or treasured ornaments. Any furniture still in one piece was stacked in the street, while the clearing-up went on. People salvaged and recycled what they could, to start a new home.

## War damage

- In London alone, over 3 million homes were destroyed or damaged.

- In the naval base of Portsmouth, 60,000 of the city's 70,000 homes were damaged.

- In Aberdeen, Scotland, 2,000 homes were damaged; in Eastbourne on the south coast of England, 3,700 homes were affected; and over 11,000 homes in Great Yarmouth on the east coast were hit.

- The town of Dover was not only bombed, but also shelled by German guns in France, 35 kilometres (22 miles) away across the Channel.

**21**

**Summer 1941**

By summer, around 500,000 bombed-out Londoners have been rehoused.

**September 1941**

Air Raid Precautions (ARP) is renamed "Civil Defence", to include the Fire Service.

**December 1941**

At least 200,000 bombs have fallen on Britain. London has reported 50,000 incidents. About 5,000 of the 44,000 people killed are under 16.

# Wardens and rescuers

During the Blitz, there were millions of civil defence workers in Britain, 80 per cent of them part-time volunteers. They included ARP wardens and rescue squads. Rescuers worked quickly but carefully, to find victims buried beneath bricks, concrete, and timber. Sadly, often the rescuers brought out only dead bodies. Badly hurt people were taken by ambulance to hospital. People fit enough to walk were helped to the nearest first-aid post.

▼ A rescue squad at work. Often rescues went on for hours, to find people trapped under the stairs – a favourite place to take shelter.

## Blitz front line

Rescue and first-aid teams were kept busy in every town and city:

- Air Raid Precautions (ARP) wardens phoned details of each bomb to a local control centre.

- The control centre sent ambulances and rescue squads to the scene.

- First-aid workers cared for the injured.

- Heavy Rescue teams worked with their hands, picks, shovels, and lifting gear to free victims trapped by rubble.

- The Women's Voluntary Service (WVS) served drinks and food to rescuers and the rescued.

Rescue workers gather for a welcome cup of tea at a WVS mobile canteen.

## Eyewitness

"... people with blackened faces were rushing in and out of houses left standing ... shouting for lost relatives. It is the usual work, collecting the less injured and applying hurried first aid. Suddenly a shout is heard: 'Quiet please'. Immediately engines stop, there is an uncanny hush as the sound detectors are used [to find people buried beneath rubble] ... three children found later, but dead. You cannot do much ..."

*This is how one rescue worker remembered the awful scene after a bomb, as people searched for survivors.*

◀ ARP wardens knew their own areas well. They were often first on the scene to report damage and take details from residents.

23

# CARRYING ON

**Bombs did not stop people working. Despite the deaths and the damage to property, the British "carried on".**

During the Blitz, people went to work on time, even after sleepless nights. They snatched a few hours of sleep whenever and wherever they could. They ate food hot when the gas and electricity were switched on, and made do with cold dinners when the power was off. Children carried on going to school – unless the school had been bombed.

## Children at war

As the air raids went on, month after month, most children began to take the Blitz for granted. They played on bomb-sites, collected bits of bombs or crashed planes as souvenirs, and invented war-games. In 1940, some children practised with catapults and bows and arrows, just in case the Germans invaded!

## Keeping things working

Buses kept running, though petrol was rationed so many private cars were shut away until after the war. Trains ran too, as damaged track and stations were quickly patched up. Emergency workers worked hard to repair broken water and gas pipes, and reconnect damaged electricity cables.

▶ Children played among the rubble of bombed buildings, and collected bits from crashed planes whenever they got the chance.

| May 1942 | 1943–1944 | 6 June 1944 |
| --- | --- | --- |
| The first "Thousand Bomber" raid. The RAF sends 1,047 bombers to attack the German city of Cologne. | Hundreds of American and British bombers attack German cities day and night. German bombing of Britain is reduced to a few small raids. | The D-Day invasion of Normandy, France. The **Allies** begin the liberation of Western Europe. |

▶ The V-1 became known as the "buzz-bomb" or "doodlebug", because it had a sputtering engine.

## Last stages of the Blitz

The worst of the Blitz came to an end in 1941, when Germany attacked the Soviet Union. However, bombing raids on Britain continued into 1944, when the Germans launched two new secret weapons: V-1 flying bombs and V-2 rockets. People could see and hear the V-1 coming; when its engine stopped, they knew it was about to fall to earth and blow up. The V-2 rocket flew too fast to be seen or heard. There was no warning, just a tremendous explosion. Fortunately, Allied armies managed to destroy or capture most V-1 and V-2 launch sites by the end of 1944, so the bombardments grew less frequent.

## Animals in the Blitz

Professor Julian Huxley studied how bombs affected animals in London Zoo.

- Camels "did not even get up when a bomb fell within ten yards".

- Parrots imitated air sirens, chimpanzees screeched at them.

- Some people claimed their dogs could hear the difference between the engines of British and German aircraft.

- Cats disappeared to find their own "air raid shelters".

## Eyewitness

An ambulance man in Birmingham noticed teenage girl helpers chatting and painting their nails. He thought, "Wait till the bombs start, then you'll be a bit more nervous." When the first bombs fell, he ran in to warn the girls, "and there they all were, just sitting there, doing their nails."

**13 June 1944**
First V-1 flying bomb lands on London.

**9 September 1944**
First V-2 rocket fired at London. On 25 November a V-2 hits a Woolworths store and kills 160 people in New Cross, London.

**8 May 1945**
VE Day – the end of the war in Europe.

# Keep smiling

**CARRYING ON**

During the Blitz, people put up with danger, shortages, and inconveniences. They felt that "we are all in this together", and made the rueful excuse: "there is a war on". This togetherness is what people mean when they talk about the "Blitz spirit".

Jokes helped people cope with fear and scary moments. Hairdressers advertised "close shaves" and "high-explosive haircuts". Shops with wrecked fronts put up notices saying "Business as usual" or "More open than normal". Newspaper cartoons poked fun at Hitler, and people made up rude rhymes and comic songs about the Nazis.

## Laugh It Off!

"Little drops of water, little grains of sand
Lots and lots of buckets, standing close at hand,
Yards and yards of hosepipe ready in the hall –
That's the stuff to give 'em when incendiaries fall!"

*A verse to keep people smiling from a wartime illustrated book called* Laugh It Off.

▲ Typical wartime song titles were "When They Sound the Last All-Clear", "When the Lights go on in London", and "Good Luck, Until We Meet Again".

## Entertainment for all

- Cinemas reopened and stayed open throughout the Blitz, as did theatres, museums, and art galleries.

- Variety shows and music concerts were held in factory canteens at lunchtimes.

- Football matches were played, even though many star players were away, fighting in the forces.

- On BBC radio, *Music While You Work* played happy tunes to get weary workers singing – and working faster.

▶ Dance halls, nightclubs, and village halls were usually packed with dancers, especially at weekends. Often the band was made up of soldiers.

▼ Cartoonists had a lot of fun with the Nazi leaders – they made them look ridiculous instead of frightening.

◀ Entertainment helped keep up people's spirits. Being together at the cinema or a theatre show helped people forget the Blitz for an hour or so.

# ALL CLEAR

After D-Day (6 June 1944), the end of the war was in sight. In September 1944, the streetlights in Britain went back on. In May 1945 the war in Europe came to an end. In August, the war against Japan ended, after the dropping of atomic bombs on two Japanese cities.

## Rebuilding Britain

The Blitz changed Britain. Old city centres and housing districts were destroyed, along with some historic buildings. After the war, there was much rebuilding to be done, to provide new homes, schools, hospitals, and factories. Derelict spaces or "bomb-sites" could still be seen in the 1950s, when high-rise flats were built to replace streets of terraced houses. By the 1960s, Coventry had a new cathedral, alongside the ruins of the old one.

## Memories of the Blitz

People who lived through the Blitz never forgot it. Their wartime experiences have been recorded, in books and on audio and video archives, for future generations. Only a few old people can now remember living through the Blitz. For them, the sound of an air raid siren still stirs memories.

▲ Prefabricated and partly prefabricated homes were put up to rehouse homeless families. Intended as temporary solution, many "prefabs" were still in use at least 20 years later.

## Facts about the bombing war

- German air raids on Britain killed more than 60,000 people.
- More than 86,000 were injured.
- Millions of British people took part in military and civil defence against air raids.
- The highest casualties in separate air raids in Europe were: Hamburg, Germany (July 1943), over 43,000 killed; and Dresden, Germany (February 1945), up to 150,000 killed.

# TIMELINE

## 1939
**1 September** Germany invades Poland. World War II begins.
**3 September** Britain and France declare war on Germany.

## 1940
**July** The Battle of Britain begins, with attacks by the German Luftwaffe on Britain.
**25 August** British planes bomb Berlin.
**7 September** German bombers switch their attacks from RAF airfields to London.
**11–26 September** Southampton experiences its first big air raid.
**15 September** The Luftwaffe suffers high losses in the Battle of Britain.
**September** People begin sleeping in the London Underground.
**14–15 November** The night Blitz on Coventry.
**19 November** Birmingham has its first big raid, with 800 "incidents" in one night.
**24 November** Bristol is hit for the first time.
**12 December** First big air raid on Sheffield.
**22–25 December** Manchester is attacked.

## 1941
**2 January** Cardiff suffers its worst raid.
**19–21 February** Swansea is attacked by up to 250 bombers.
**13–14 March** Over 400 German planes bomb Clydeside in Scotland.
**March** RAF night fighters are equipped with radar, to track German bombers.
**15 April** Belfast is targeted by over 100 planes.
**21–29 April** Plymouth is raided by up to 700 planes.
**1–7 May** Up to 800 German planes bomb Merseyside.
**10–11 May** More than 1400 people are killed by bombs in London's worst night of bombing.
**22 June** Germany invades the Soviet Union.
**September** Air Raid Precautions is renamed Civil Defence.
**7 December** Japanese planes attack Pearl Harbor, Hawaii.
**8 December** The United States, Britain, Australia, and Canada declare war on Japan.

## 1942
**15 February** The important British naval base at Singapore is captured by Japanese forces. The Japanese bomb northern Australia.
**3 March** The RAF's new Lancaster heavy bombers go into action.
**July** First US B-17 bombers arrive in Britain.

## 1943
**28 February** RAF bombs Berlin. Allies step up raids on Germany, the RAF at night and the Americans by day, with fighters escorting bombers.
**February** Last Germans at Stalingrad surrender, marking the end of the German advance into the Soviet Union.
**May** Allies drive German and Italian forces out of North Africa.
**July** Allied bombers devastate the city of Hamburg, Germany.
**3 September** Italy surrenders, after Allied forces invade from Sicily.

## 1944
**18–26 February** Heaviest raids on London since 1941.
**20 February** US bombers attack German aircraft factories. Yet German production actually increases.
**6 June** D-Day. Allied armies invade France to begin the liberation of Western Europe.
**13 June** The first German V-1 flying bomb hits London.
**25 August** The Allies enter liberated Paris, France's capital city.
**9 September** The first German V-2 rocket lands on London.

## 1945
**13/14 February** Allied bombers devastate the German city of Dresden.
**March** The last German V-2 rocket falls on London.
**30 April** Hitler kills himself as Soviet armies close in on Berlin.
**2 May** Berlin is captured by Soviet armies.
**7 May** Germany surrenders.
**8 May** VE or Victory in Europe Day.
**6 August** Allies drop an atomic bomb on Hiroshima. A second destroys Nagasaki on 9 August.
**14 August** VJ (Victory over Japan) Day ends the war.

# GLOSSARY

**air raid** attack on a target by aircraft dropping bombs

**air raid shelter** building or structure designed to protect people from bombs

**Allies** nations united in an alliance to fight Germany, Italy, Japan, and their allies during World War II. The Allies include the United Kingdom, Australia, New Zealand, South Africa, and Canada, as well as the United States, Soviet Union, France, and Poland.

**atomic bomb** weapon using nuclear fission. The A-bomb dropped on Hiroshima in 1945 was more powerful than 12,000 tonnes of high explosive.

**Blitz** short for *Blitzkrieg*, German for "lightning war". In Britain, the term was used to describe the bombing of towns and cities.

**bomber** plane built to fly long distances and drop various kinds of bombs

**civil defence** protecting civilians from attack in wartime

**corrugated steel** extra strong sheets of metal

**dogfight** airborne fight between fighter planes

**evacuate** move people from a dangerous area to places where they will be safe

**gas mask** breathing apparatus worn on the face to protect a person from the effects of breathing in harmful substances in the air

**gramophone** machine for playing records

**incendiary** small bomb containing chemicals that burn on landing, starting fires

**morale** fighting spirit, a belief that your side will win

**Nazis** members of the National Socialist German Workers' Party, led by Adolf Hitler

**propaganda** selected information published in the media so as to show your own side in a good light and the enemy in a bad way

**radar** use of radio waves to detect distant objects, such as aircraft. It was invented in the 1930s when it was called "radiolocation".

**siren** device used to make a wailing sound, to tell people that an air raid is expected, or over

**squadron** unit in an air force, usually made up of about 12–20 aeroplanes, their pilots, and supporting crew

**stick** group of bombs dropped from an aircraft

**wireless** 1940s term for a radio set

# FINDING OUT MORE

If you are interested in finding out more about World War II, here are some more books and websites you might find useful.

## Further reading

Your local public library's adult section should have plenty of war books, including books about what it was like to live through the Blitz. Written by people who were actually there, such books will give you an idea of what ordinary people thought about the war and their part in it.

## Books for younger readers

*Britain at War: Air Raids,* Martin Parson (Wayland, 1999)

*Causes and Consequences of the Second World War,* Stewart Ross (Evans, 2003)

*Causes of World War II,* Paul Dowswell (Heinemann Library, 2002)

*Going to War in World War II,* Moira Butterfield (Franklin Watts, 2001)

*History Through Poetry; World War II,* Reg Grant (Hodder Wayland, 2001)

*The Day the War was Won,* Colin Hymion (Ticktock Media, 2003)

*World in Flames: In the Air,* Peter Hepplewhite (Macmillan Children's Books, 2001)

*World in Flames: On Land,* Neil Tonge (Macmillan Children's Books, 2001)

*WW2 Stories: War at Home,* Anthony Masters (Franklin Watts, 2004)

*WW2 Stories: War in the Air,* Anthony Masters (Franklin Watts, 2004)

*WW2 True Stories,* Clive Gifford (Hodder Children's Books, 2002)

## Websites

http://www.iwm.org.uk/ – the website of the Imperial War Museum in London.

http://www.wartimememories.co.uk/ – a website containing wartime recollections, including those of people who lived through the Blitz.

http://bbc.co.uk/history/war/wwtwo/ – this website from the BBC has lots of resources about World War II.

# INDEX

# Titles in the *World At War* series include:

Hardback: 0-431-10376-3

Hardback: 0-431-10380-1

Hardback: 0-431-10377-1

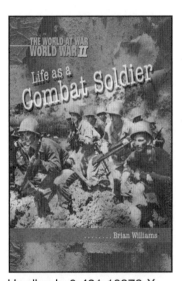

Hardback: 0-431-10378-X

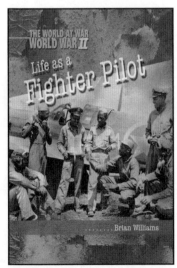

Hardback: 0-431-10379-8

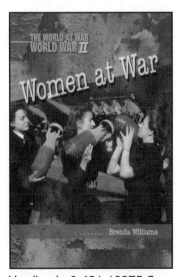

Hardback: 0-431-10375-5

Find out about other titles from Heinemann Library on our website www.heinemann.co.uk/library